Restless

Devotional & Workbook for Struggling Fathers

Introduction

I created this devotional because I needed it. I was desperate to find some kind of comfort and help as a father facing a custody battle and divorce, and I couldn't find anything geared toward me. While I began to write this for myself, I also started sending it to a father-friend of mine who was facing the same issues I was. His confirmations back on each day were all I needed to see to understand that this needed to be shared.

I am in the middle of yet another sleepless night where I woke up and began thinking about all of the heartache these past two years have wrought. Writing this introduction after all of the devotionals have been selected and compiled forced me to relive the purpose behind the words. I am reminded that there is no promise of easiness on this side of heaven.

Yet, these very devotionals that chronicle a myriad of feelings while dealing with divorce, a custody battle, and financial woes still prove a beautiful constant: God will bring you through it. Now, He might have to drag you through the mire and thickets to get you where you're going, but He is faithful to do it.

Fatherhood is the hardest responsibility that we are granted in this life. When it undergoes stress and threat, we often do not react with grace and mercy. Yet, our Father displays those gifts to us consistently. He immediately provides the example that we should realign ourselves to reflect.

As I said, we are not promised *easy*. Every day that we wake up is another example of us getting through it. Don't lose out on the love of your children, and the support of those around you. Despite the destruction that may be taking place, take heart that there is also construction happening. It is these kinds of trials that either force us into stronger fatherhood or give us the excuse to cower away and dissolve. I pray that for each of us, it would be the former.

Day 1

Guard Your Heart

Guard your heart diligently, for from it flow the springs of life.
Proverbs 4:23 TLV

Notes

_____

_____

_____

_____

_____

_____

_____

_____

_____

_____

_____

_____

_____

_____

_____

_____

There are moments in life that leave you feeling like you were a crash test dummy that just failed an experiment pretty hard. Twisted in the heaps of metal, plastic, and cloth lay a body that used to carry you through all of the highs of life.

Divorce is a lot like that car whose parts failed and, somehow, the technician forgot to install brakes. Custody battles are not unlike the large brick wall that, what's left of, the broken vehicle is splayed out in front of.

These matters of the heart are some of the hardest things any human can face. Without keeping guard in these times, you may end up causing even more damage. Anger, bitterness, resentment, and depression can easily seep in. Even still, finding the will to check on your own condition might be a heroic task.

It's important to take the time and put effort into the healing process. How grateful should we be that The Creator honours a guarded heart? When you begin to make the repairs and mend the pieces back together; it might not look perfect but it can be whole again. Do the best thing that you can do, submit your heart back to Him and watch what He can do with it. This is when The Creator reignites the springs of life, which can carry you through to the fulfillment of His purpose for all this mess.

Remember in your prayers today:

Teach me your ways, Adonai. Take the shattered pieces of my heart and help me to put them back together, so that I may find the springs of life again to better serve Your will.

Introspection and Prayer

- **Reflection Questions**: Reflect on personal struggles and worries.
- **Action Item**: Write a prayer, focusing on seeking comfort and guidance.

_____

_____

_____

_____

_____

_____

_____

_____

_____

_____

_____

_____

_____

_____

_____

_____

_____

_____

_____

_____

_____

_____

_____

_____

_____

Other passages to read about the heart:

"Out of the good treasure of his heart the good man brings forth good, and out of evil the evil man brings forth evil. For from the overflow of the heart his mouth speaks." Luke 6:45 (TLV)

"*Shalom* I leave you, My *shalom* I give to you; but not as the world gives! Do not let your heart be troubled or afraid."
John 14:27 (TLV)

"And hope does not disappoint, because God's love has been poured into our hearts through the *Ruach ha-Kodesh* who was given to us."Romans 5:5 (TLV)

Day 2

Hold on to Your Anger

Fathers, do not provoke your children to anger, but bring them up in the discipline and instruction of the Lord.
Ephesians 6:4 TLV

Notes

_____

_____

_____

_____

_____

_____

_____

_____

_____

_____

_____

_____

_____

_____

_____

I have only ever met one or two men who do not struggle with issues of anger. In this current circumstance, you may feel a boiling rage deep within you. It may even be justified. Fighting for the things you had built up that are being taken away, and fighting for time with the children that you love can lead to feelings of justifiable anger. Even still, and even with my understanding; a bigger work is at hand.

Your children need you to teach them the reality of a calm heart. The turmoil that you might be feeling might only further the struggles that your children are facing. Showing them your anger teaches them that it is logical for them to show anger. You are still their parent, even in your struggles. You still owe them your best. God is not pleased when his children are harmed. Our responsibility as fathers should always overtake our quickness to lean into our temper.

One of the ways children learn how to deal with and react to, situations is as a reflection of their parent's actions. They are always watching, and absorbing their environment. Show them your reliance on God, rather than yourself.

Remember in your prayers today:

Calm my anger, Adonai. Help me to be the example that you have called me to be.

Overcoming Anger

- **Exercise**: Identify instances where anger was a challenge and explore healthier ways to address it.
- **Discussion Point**: Share insights on managing anger with a support group or journal.

_____
_____
_____
_____
_____
_____
_____
_____
_____
_____
_____
_____
_____
_____
_____
_____
_____
_____
_____
_____
_____
_____
_____
_____
_____

Other passages to read when feeling angry:

"Be angry, yet do not sin. Do not let the sun go down on your anger..." Ephesians 4:26 (TLV)

"Know this, my dear brothers and sisters: let every person be quick to listen, slow to speak, and slow to anger— for human anger doesn't produce the righteousness of God." James 1:19-20 (TLV)

"A fool gives full vent to his temper, but a wise man holds it back." Proverbs 29:11 (TLV)

Day 3

Integrity at all Costs

A righteous person walks in integrity.
Blessed are his children after him.
Proverbs 20:7 TLV

Notes

_____

_____

_____

_____

_____

_____

_____

_____

_____

_____

_____

_____

_____

_____

_____

I can only imagine that every person strives to live, and love, with integrity. When relationships fail, however, the true nature of wickedness creeps up in our hearts. Integrity becomes one of the first major internal battlegrounds. We feel right and justified in our responses to pain.

We struggle with the questions of "How could my ex be so wrong and why am I the one who has to suffer for it?" When in reality, we do plenty of things wrong consistently in our day to day. Regardless of our feelings of righteous indignation, our integrity must be what elevates to the surface. Slipping into anger or depression robs a blessing from us, and our children.

God makes it plain that we are never to give in to the feelings of our flesh. This is in stark contrast to our inner desire for self-justification and preservation. I understand how chaotically difficult this time in life can be, but remember that we are called for a purpose.

Remember in your prayers today:

Adonai, quicken my heart to remember that You are the God of blessings. Remind me that these trials can be the proving grounds for my purpose.

Moving Forward

- **Activity**: List personal goals and steps to achieve them, emphasizing moving forward from past struggles.
- **Prayer Focus**: Pray for strength to overcome past pains and move forward.

Other passages to read about integrity:

"The integrity of the upright guides them, but the crookedness of the treacherous will destroy them." Proverbs 11:3

"Yet with humility and reverence—keeping a clear conscience so that, whatever you are accused of, those who abuse you for your good conduct in Messiah may be put to shame." 1 Peter 3:16 (TLV)

"We have regard for what is honorable—not only before the Lord, but also before people." 2 Corinthians 8:21 (TLV)

Day 4

Worry Wart

Cast all your worries on Him, for He cares for you
1 Peter 5:7 TLV

Notes

_____
_____
_____
_____
_____
_____
_____
_____
_____
_____
_____
_____
_____
_____
_____
_____
_____
_____
_____

When going through the treacherous landscape of divorce and custody fights, every day can feel like it is leaning into worry. Will the next email from a lawyer be destructive? Maybe by some chance, it will be a simple correspondence. Will the unread message from my ex be an attack on my character or a statement that I wouldn't be able to see my child (or children) that weekend? It could just be a possible update on their grades or a new development.

On top of those kinds of worries, you may be facing battles of lost property, finding a home, a change in jobs, a dwindling social circle, etc.... All of the hard things in life don't subside just because you are facing new struggles.

There is someone who doesn't mind hearing about all of it. In fact, He cares to listen. What's more, is that He is also the one who can help you change your circumstances. This might not look like our idea of "fixing the problems", but sometimes it is a moment of calm. Other times it is an answer to a question that has been plaguing your thoughts. It may even be a clear closing (or opening) of a door. He loves us enough to not only hear our worries but to help us deal with them.

Remember in your prayers today:

Thank You, Yeshua, for being a source of comfort and camaraderie. Let me never forget Your ability to overcome every obstacle and the realization that I can do the same through You.

Embracing God's Mercy

- **Journal Prompt**: Write about a time when you experienced mercy and how it impacted you.
- **Group Discussion or Reflection**: How can we show mercy to others?

_____
_____
_____
_____
_____
_____
_____
_____
_____
_____
_____
_____
_____
_____
_____
_____
_____
_____
_____
_____
_____
_____
_____
_____

Other passages to read when feeling worried:

"So I say to you, do not worry about your life—what you will eat or drink, or about your body, what you will wear. Isn't life more than food and the body more than clothing?" Matthew 6:25 (TLV)

"Fear not, for I am with you,
be not dismayed, for I am your God.
I will strengthen you.
Surely I will help you.
I will uphold you with My righteous right hand." Isaiah 41:10 (TLV)

"For God has not given us a spirit of timidity but of power and love and self-discipline." 2 Timothy 1:7 (TLV)

Day 5

Hotheaded but Cool-Spirited

Be angry, yet do not sin.
Do not let the sun go down on your anger,
Ephesians 4:26 TLV

Notes

_____
_____
_____
_____
_____
_____
_____
_____
_____
_____
_____
_____
_____
_____
_____
_____
_____
_____

I remember being told so many times over the course of engagement and marriage that you should never go to bed angry. I also know that I definitely did go to bed angry. I could take a guess and bet that many others did as well.

The effort should be taken to resolve the upset, and that is the major takeaway from the second sentence of this devotional passage. Unresolved issues breed resentment and can widen the chasm between the parties.

The first sentence of the passage is arguably the harder section. Sin may sound like it encapsulates a smaller set of rules... But the essence of the scripture teaches us to not let our anger result in any action that would separate us from God or His purpose for us.

How grateful should we be that God understands we will be angry? It is not a foreign concept and is an emotion even shown by God himself. However, there is no excuse to act out with aggression.

Remember in your prayers today:

Thank you for acknowledging our emotions, and being the reason that we can overcome them.

Combatting Envy

- **Activity**: Identify situations where envy arises and devise strategies to counter it.
- **Reflection**: Consider how focusing on God's plan can alleviate feelings of envy.

_____
_____
_____
_____
_____
_____
_____
_____
_____
_____
_____
_____
_____
_____
_____
_____
_____
_____
_____
_____
_____
_____
_____
_____

Other passages to read when feeling angry:

"Be angry, yet do not sin. Do not let the sun go down on your anger..." Ephesians 4:26 (TLV)

"Know this, my dear brothers and sisters: let every person be quick to listen, slow to speak, and slow to anger— for human anger doesn't produce the righteousness of God." James 1:19-20 (TLV)

"A fool gives full vent to his temper, but a wise man holds it back." Proverbs 29:11 (TLV)

Day 6

Forward, Not Backward

Whenever I remember, my soul is downcast within me.
Lamentations 3:20 TLV

Notes

_____

_____

_____

_____

_____

_____

_____

_____

_____

_____

_____

_____

_____

_____

_____

_____

_____

_____

_____

_____

I am a big believer in using Scripture with context. I also believe that establishing a point based on a singular scripture can be useful under the right circumstances. Lamentations chapter three is a heartache of a chapter, and it surely won't leave anyone feeling uplifted and encouraged.

With that being said, verse 20 stands out to me for the realization of the pain that memories can cause. Within the confines of the purpose of these devotions, we may remember pain from arguments in relationships. Or, perhaps, those little quips that got said just to try and get under your skin. Maybe you even find pain in remembering the things you said, or did, that caused issues.

It is surely not God's desire for us to be stuck in our memories, or trapped in our past. He is a God of future glory, that we get to access in the here and now. The best piece of encouragement I could offer anyone battling painful memories is to repent. That's right, confess the reality of those memories, and ask to be forgiven in the parts where you might have caused division or destruction. Then, forgive yourself, get out there, and do what is right.

Remember in your prayers today:

Forgive me for my failures to exhibit your mercy and grace. Thank You for the peace in knowing that You desire for Your children to move forward, and not to stay stuck in our pasts.

Body Image and Faith

- **Exercise**: Reflect on personal body image perceptions and how faith influences these views.
- **Discussion**: How does faith shape our understanding of physical appearance?

_____

_____

_____

_____

_____

_____

_____

_____

_____

_____

_____

_____

_____

_____

_____

_____

_____

_____

_____

_____

_____

_____

_____

Other passages to read about perseverance:

"Seek *Adonai* and His strength. Seek His face always."
1 Chronicles 16:11 (TLV)

"So let us not lose heart in doing good, for in due time we will reap if we don't give up." Galatians 6:9 (TLV)

"For we have become partners of Messiah, if we hold our original conviction firm until the end." Hebrews 3:14 (TLV)

Day 7

The Hard Times

But the mercy of Adonai is from everlasting to everlasting on those who revere Him, His righteousness to children's children,
Psalms 103:17 TLV

Notes

_____
_____
_____
_____
_____
_____
_____
_____
_____
_____
_____
_____
_____
_____
_____
_____
_____
_____
_____

It's hard to not recognize the impact of the hardest days. They can take such a toll on your mind and heart. There have been moments over the past year and a half where I have just wanted to shut off my phone and stay in bed. Ultimately, it is nothing but a delay tactic.

As children of God, we are given an amazing gift called mercy. Our Creator cares about our struggles and our pain; even if some of it may have been brought on by our own actions.

Mercy is showing compassion while in a position that could allow you to cause pain. How lucky are we that He hears our voices? He has no desire to hurt us, but rather to walk with us as we face the day.

In the way that He shows us mercy, we too should show it to our children. Just as we are not perfect, our children are not either. Our positions should never be utilized to inflict pain. Instead, we are called to lead by example; we receive mercy, and we show mercy.

Remember in your prayers today:

Teach me to remember the blessing of mercy that you have shown me. I pray that the same mercy will follow me through all of the days ahead.

Cultivating Self-Discipline

- **Challenge**: Set a personal goal requiring discipline (e.g., daily prayer, reading scripture) and track progress.
- **Reflection Question:** How does self-discipline in small areas impact larger aspects of life?

_____
_____
_____
_____
_____
_____
_____
_____
_____
_____
_____
_____
_____
_____
_____
_____
_____
_____
_____
_____
_____
_____
_____
_____
_____

Other passages to read about perseverance:

"Seek ADONAI and His strength. Seek His face always."
1 Chronicles 16:11 (TLV)

"So let us not lose heart in doing good, for in due time we will reap if we don't give up." Galatians 6:9 (TLV)

"For we have become partners of Messiah, if we hold our original conviction firm until the end." Hebrews 3:14 (TLV)

Day 8

Not on Their Level

Do not be overcome by evil, but overcome evil with good.
Romans 12:21 TLV

Notes

_____

_____

_____

_____

_____

_____

_____

_____

_____

_____

_____

_____

_____

_____

_____

_____

_____

_____

Do you ever feel like just snapping on everything and everyone? Oh, how good would it feel to really give people a piece of your mind? You could finally get all that anger and pent-up agression out into the open. Leave it for everyone else to sort out!

I understand how difficult it can be to keep holding things back. There have been moments throughout these trials where I felt like I really had a good point... But it would require me to sink down into an evil level.

God promises us peace when we ask for it, but what He isn't willing to give us is vengeance by our own hand. I find myself constantly trying to remember that I don't know what anyone else is going through in their time alone. I have no idea if God is dealing with them, or if they are floundering in their own turmoil.

What I can do, is pray for goodness to overcome evil. From this desire, God pours life, peace, and understanding into us. We should never desire to "have it our way" and lean into the darkness, but we should shine a light on those weaknesses and let God correct our hearts.

Remember in your prayers today:

Quench my vengeful heart, Adonai. Teach me to continue in your ways, which are good. Strengthen me to fight against evil.

Handling Temptation

- **Activity**: Journal about recent temptations and how they were handled.
- **Prayer Focus**: Seek guidance in managing future temptations.

Other passages to read when feeling angry:

"Be angry, yet do not sin. Do not let the sun go down on your anger…" Ephesians 4:26 (TLV)

"Know this, my dear brothers and sisters: let every person be quick to listen, slow to speak, and slow to anger— for human anger doesn't produce the righteousness of God." James 1:19-20 (TLV)

"A fool gives full vent to his temper, but a wise man holds it back." Proverbs 29:11 (TLV)

Day 9

Dad Bod

So I say to you, do not worry about your life—what you will eat or drink, or about your body, what you will wear. Isn't life more than food and the body more than clothing?
Matthew 6:25 TLV

Notes

_____

_____

_____

_____

_____

_____

_____

_____

_____

_____

_____

_____

_____

_____

If you are blessed enough to have a dad bod, then today's passage might hit harder for you. This is one of those verses that could be taken so completely out of context and flipped into justification for any variety of things we shouldn't be doing with (or to) our bodies.

Yet, within the context of the surrounding verses, we learn something so important about love. As men of God, we are called to be providers. This means for our children, for the women in our lives, and even for those less fortunate than us. That can be a hard pill to swallow sometimes.

In moments like these, as I sit here writing this while in the middle of a custody battle, looking for a job, completely unsure of where God's plan takes me next; this passage reminds me that I am taken care of. In fact, it is vital to remember passages like this in these moments. Consider the very next verse:

Look at the birds of the air. They do not sow or reap or gather into barns; yet your Father in heaven feeds them. Are you not of more value than they? - Matthew 6:26 TLV

We are so loved, and should never forget it. Even when the lights are shut off and it feels like we are just stumbling in the darkness, He is still planning ahead for us. What greater comfort is there than to know that the Creator loves our dad bods?

Remember in your prayers today:

I thank you, Lord, for sustaining me and having a plan for my life. Teach me to walk after you, to be the provider you have called me to be; just as You provide for me.

Parental Influence

- **Discussion or Journal**: Reflect on the impact of parental influence on children, focusing on spiritual guidance.
- **Exercise**: Create a plan to incorporate faith into daily parenting practices.

Other passages to read about integrity:

"The integrity of the upright guides them, but the crookedness of the treacherous will destroy them." Proverbs 11:3

"Yet with humility and reverence—keeping a clear conscience so that, whatever you are accused of, those who abuse you for your good conduct in Messiah may be put to shame." 1 Peter 3:16 (TLV)

"We have regard for what is honorable—not only before the Lord, but also before people." 2 Corinthians 8:21 (TLV)

Day 10

Check Your Spirit

For God has not given us a spirit of timidity but of power and love and self-discipline.
2 Timothy 1:7 TLV

Notes

_____

_____

_____

_____

_____

_____

_____

_____

_____

_____

_____

_____

_____

_____

_____

_____

Power and *love* are not terms that are typically seen used together…unless you are a 70's rock music fan. I love when scripture takes ideas and flips our perspective of them. God has called us to be bold and powerful, but with love.

This is a concept that is the opposite of what we see in the world. So many are taught to scream, yell, and fight to have their point pushed forward. When I consider Yeshua and his disciples, however, I see a clear contrast. Their message was powerful, and everywhere they went they found new people who were willing to listen. Their message was of love, hope, and faith. They were living under Roman rule! Not only that, but they were angering the religious leaders everywhere they went!

Imagine speaking with love even when everyone else around you is egging you on to fight. This is where self-discipline comes in. We constantly have to keep check of our spirit and make sure that we are allowing love to stamp out anger. Your power can be used for good, or for evil. Yeshua could have disintegrated every person who stood against him…but instead, he spoke firmly to them, with a hand of love always outstretched. Nothing makes the darkness angrier than when it is illuminated by love.

Remember in your prayers today:

Quicken my spirit to operate in love, just as You did.

Embracing God's Plan

- **Reflection Exercise**: Analyze areas of life where self-made plans have fallen short, and how trusting in God's plan could change outcomes.
- **Group Discussion or Journaling**: The importance of surrendering personal plans to God.

_____
_____
_____
_____
_____
_____
_____
_____
_____
_____
_____
_____
_____
_____
_____
_____
_____
_____
_____
_____
_____
_____
_____
_____

Other passages to read about the heart:

"Out of the good treasure of his heart the good man brings forth good, and out of evil the evil man brings forth evil. For from the overflow of the heart his mouth speaks." Luke 6:45 (TLV)

"*Shalom* I leave you, My *shalom* I give to you; but not as the world gives! Do not let your heart be troubled or afraid."
John 14:27 (TLV)

"And hope does not disappoint, because God's love has been poured into our hearts through the *Ruach ha-Kodesh* who was given to us."Romans 5:5 (TLV)

Day 11

You are my Praise

Heal me, Adonai, and I will be healed. Save me, and I will be saved. For You are my praise.
Jeremiah 17:14 TLV

Notes

_____

_____

_____

_____

_____

_____

_____

_____

_____

_____

_____

_____

_____

_____

_____

_____

_____

In the New Testament we find passage after passage of people coming to know Yeshua because of the works, signs, and miracles that He performed. Even with the disciples, He had to remind them on multiple occasions that the point of all of this was salvation, not a miracle.

Within the context of the Old Testament, we find pleas for healing and deliverance. There were sacrifices to be made, there were rituals to acknowledge and perform.

We are so truly blessed that we are able to reach out to Him without the confines of traditionalism. He is there to hear our cries for help, and for salvation, and even just simple conversation. There is no more veil to keep us from His presence. When we are struggling, our peace is just a call away. If anger is welling up in our hearts, He is there to calm us down.

However, let's quit trying to utilize Him for what He can do for us and instead make him our praise for no other reason than His glory. This kind of approach leaves room for Him to work in us the way He wants to, not according to our desires.

Remember in your prayers today:

Adonai, You are holy. Thank You for Your presence, and for lending an ear to my prayers. Let me never replace Your glorification with my needs. Have Your way.

Overcoming Jealousy

- **Activity**: Identify moments of jealousy and explore their roots.
- **Prayer Focus**: Seek help in overcoming jealousy and fostering contentment.

_____

_____

_____

_____

_____

_____

_____

_____

_____

_____

_____

_____

_____

_____

_____

_____

_____

_____

_____

_____

_____

_____

_____

_____

Other passages to read about thankfulness:

"I will praise *ADONAI* with my whole heart. I will tell about all Your wonders." Psalm 9:25 (TLV)

"I praise You in the great assembly, acclaiming You among a throng of people." Psalm 35:18 (TLV)

"Therefore as you received Messiah *Yeshua* as Lord, so continue to walk in Him—rooted and built up in Him and established in your faith just as you were taught, overflowing with thankfulness." Colossians 2:6-7 (TLV)

Day 12

It Ends Sometime

Better the end of a matter than its beginning. Better a patient spirit than a proud one.
Ecclesiastes 7:8 TLV

Notes

_____

_____

_____

_____

_____

_____

_____

_____

_____

_____

_____

_____

_____

_____

_____

_____

_____

Patience and pride: two elements contained in every human being that is constantly at war. Pride urges you to act on impulse, to stand up for yourself and how epically awesome you are. It elevates our hero complex, placing us in the central role of our own epic quests.

Patience, on the other hand, often tells us to shut up. It wants us to take a back seat and wait for clarity. It is antithetical to our nature, and our comfort zones.

Today's passage is teaching us to step back and let the situations take their course. Through your patience, you will receive peace and understanding. Pride keeps us active in circumstances that are unhealthy for us. Patience allows us to observe, and heal.

I understand that this might be a hard one to grasp, as I know it is for me. However, what an atmospheric shift this passage can provide us! God is not about chaos and confusion and desires us to be peacemakers. We can do this through patience, even if we have to bite our tongues.

Remember in your prayers today:

Teach me to quench my pride, Adonai. Remind me to be patient, and to rely on your words.

Practicing Patience

- **Exercise**: Set a daily patience challenge and record experiences.
- **Reflection**: How does practicing patience impact your spiritual life and relationships?

Other passages to read about perseverance:

"Seek *Adonai* and His strength. Seek His face always."
1 Chronicles 16:11 (TLV)

"So let us not lose heart in doing good, for in due time we will reap if we don't give up." Galatians 6:9 (TLV)

"For we have become partners of Messiah, if we hold our original conviction firm until the end." Hebrews 3:14 (TLV)

Day 13

The Shaking

Cast your burden on Adonai, and He will sustain you. He will never let the righteous be shaken.
Psalms 55:23 TLV

Notes

_____
_____
_____
_____
_____
_____
_____
_____
_____
_____
_____
_____
_____
_____
_____
_____

Righteousness should be the hearts desire for any person who desires a closer relationship with God. The pursuit of righteousness comes with benefits of its own. One of them is the ability to be sustained. His presence can override the harshest circumstances, and the darkest moments.

The Lord desires our servitude, and He offers to carry the weight that we cannot bear.

The idea that the righteous cannot be shaken is the harder element of this passage to grapple with. In times like now, I can't say that things feel stable, sturdy, and held together. This passage seems to be an assurance that if God is taking care of your burdens, they will not bring you to the point of complete collapse. Even if the wind is blowing, your house won't collapse. You may need to deal with some broken windows and debris, but still you stand. There is nothing quite like the mercy that God shows when we are struggling most.

Remember in your prayers today:

Thank You for your mercy, and the ability that only You have to keep me held together.

Finding Peace in Trials

- **Journal Prompt:** Write about a recent trial and how you found peace.
- **Group Sharing or Reflection**: Discuss how faith provides peace in difficult times.

(blank lined writing space)

Other passages to read when you feel like giving up:

"So let us not lose heart in doing good, for in due time we will reap if we don't give up." Galatians 6:9 (TLV)

"Therefore, since we have such a great cloud of witnesses surrounding us, let us also get rid of every weight and entangling sin. Let us run with endurance the race set before us..."
Hebrews 12:1 (TLV)

"I can do all things through Messiah who strengthens me."
Philippians 4:13 (TLV)

Day 14

An Amazing Race

Consider it all joy, my brethren, when you encounter various trials, knowing that the testing of your faith produces endurance. And let endurance have its perfect work, so that you may be perfect and complete, lacking in nothing.
Jacob (James) 1:2-4 TLV

Notes

_____
_____
_____
_____
_____
_____
_____
_____
_____
_____
_____
_____
_____

I sat in an attorney's office today, knowing that I was once again going to have to discuss things that bother my heart. I know that, in the end, truth will hold a greater place than anything that I can conceptualize on my own. No matter how things play out, I know that I am in a race after Yeshua.

What I am finding the hardest element is the seemingly endless side to the race. At times it feels like it would be easier to just throw my hands up and say "That's it, I am out of strength." Yet, there is something deeper within me that continues to propel me forward.

I have found depths to my faith that I didn't know existed. The more pressure that gets applied, the more I have to rely on those times of lament; recognizing that there is no way I can do this myself. I find comfort in realizing that it is the constant push that drives a more active faith. How many seem to let God fall to the wayside when things get difficult? I urge you to run to God first before it would ever become a last resort.

Remember in your prayers today:

Teach me to rely on You, and not on my own strength.

Endurance in Faith

- **Activity**: Reflect on a long-term challenge and how faith has provided endurance.
- **Discussion or Journaling**: Share insights on maintaining faith in prolonged difficulties.

_____
_____
_____
_____
_____
_____
_____
_____
_____
_____
_____
_____
_____
_____
_____
_____
_____
_____
_____
_____
_____
_____
_____
_____
_____
_____
_____

Other passages to read about perseverance:

"Seek ADONAI and His strength. Seek His face always."
1 Chronicles 16:11 (TLV)

"So let us not lose heart in doing good, for in due time we will reap if we don't give up." Galatians 6:9 (TLV)

"For we have become partners of Messiah, if we hold our original conviction firm until the end." Hebrews 3:14 (TLV)

Day 15

Everywhere I Turn

No temptation has taken hold of you except what is common to mankind. But God is faithful—He will not allow you to be tempted beyond what you can handle. But with the temptation He will also provide a way of escape, so you will be able to endure it.
1 Corinthians 10:13 TLV

Notes

_____
_____
_____
_____
_____
_____
_____
_____
_____
_____
_____
_____
_____
_____

In seasons of life such as these, we will surely stumble into temptation. It comes with the territory and is part of our life experience. Everything is a training ground for the Lord. It is never promised to be easy, which fights against our self-preservation mindset.

However, God is calling us to rely on Him, even in our temptations. You can read it plainly in Scripture, that God is able to not only give us a way to flee from temptation, but a way to endure its persistent influence.

We serve a God who leads by example, and He did so by showing us that we can overcome (as shown in Matthew 4). We can find power then, that He is willing to guide us through our issues of life.

This devotional I really want to stick with you, because it comes up constantly. I challenge you to do a self-accountability check and see if it can be proven true. How many times were you tempted today? How many times did you hand it over to God and let Him help? If you didn't, did you fall into the temptation?

It may not be comfortable to do this kind of exercise, but it will prove the point of reliance on God. Stay strong, and keep up your accountability.

Remember in your prayers today:

Remind me daily, Lord, to lean on you and not my own understanding. I thank you that in my weakness, you are strong.

Coping with Temptation

- **Exercise**: Record instances of temptation and strategies used to cope.
- **Prayer Focus**: Seek strength to resist future temptations.

_____

_____

_____

_____

_____

_____

_____

_____

_____

_____

_____

_____

_____

_____

_____

_____

_____

_____

_____

_____

_____

_____

_____

Other passages to read when you feel like giving up:

"So let us not lose heart in doing good, for in due time we will reap if we don't give up." Galatians 6:9 (TLV)

"Therefore, since we have such a great cloud of witnesses surrounding us, let us also get rid of every weight and entangling sin. Let us run with endurance the race set before us..." Hebrews 12:1 (TLV)

"I can do all things through Messiah who strengthens me." Philippians 4:13 (TLV)

Day 16

Raise Them Up

Train up a child in the way he should go, when he is old he will not turn from it.
Proverbs 22:6 TLV

Notes

_____
_____
_____
_____
_____
_____
_____
_____
_____
_____
_____
_____
_____
_____
_____
_____

One of the most challenging things a human can do is try and raise other humans to be good, kind, and faithful. It can be difficult when we are facing issues that make us feel like we are less than good, kind, or faithful. Nevertheless, God places that responsibility on our shoulders as a parent. It is not a responsibility that should be taken lightly, either. How we raise a child has long-lasting effects that will carry over into adulthood. Consider the amount of individuals in counseling to help deal with how they were raised.

In every aspect of life, we must remember that our children are watching. We are their examples, more than anyone else in their lives. A healthy parent-child relationship grants you a place of influence that should be nurtured. In a world that is set on removing the integral element of faith, we have the opportunity to show them what God has done for us. Especially in these seasons of life, they can watch how we come out stronger, bolder, and with more fervor for God's presence.

We are the light of the world that our children see. What's equally important to remember is that we could also be the darkness that they see. It is a responsibility that is heavy to carry, but the reward is carried on through generations. The greatest legacy that we could leave behind is found in a child who grows up to honor the Lord.

Remember in your prayers today:

Thank you, Adonai, for the blessing of children. Remind me of my responsibility, and that in all things I should honor you. Keep Your hand over their lives, and show them the power of Your love.

Raising Children in Faith

- **Discussion or Journaling:** Share thoughts on the importance of instilling faith in children.
- **Activity:** Plan a family faith-based activity or discussion.

_____
_____
_____
_____
_____
_____
_____
_____
_____
_____
_____
_____
_____
_____
_____
_____
_____
_____
_____
_____
_____
_____
_____
_____
_____

Other passages to read about integrity:

"The integrity of the upright guides them, but the crookedness of the treacherous will destroy them." Proverbs 11:3

"Yet with humility and reverence—keeping a clear conscience so that, whatever you are accused of, those who abuse you for your good conduct in Messiah may be put to shame." 1 Peter 3:16 (TLV)

"We have regard for what is honorable—not only before the Lord, but also before people." 2 Corinthians 8:21 (TLV)

Day 17

Planmaker

Commit whatever you do to Adonai, and your plans will succeed.
Proverbs 16:3 TLV

Notes

_____

_____

_____

_____

_____

_____

_____

_____

_____

_____

_____

_____

_____

_____

_____

_____

_____

_____

_____

As parents, we are constantly either making plans or the recipients of plans that we are forced into participating in. In our personal lives, we have goals and dreams that we have at least rationalized in our minds with some plans. In our jobs, we make plans to either get a promotion, or as small as just making it through another day of work. In our social lives, we make plans to spend time with others, to go out and experience the world outside of our windows.

What I constantly am learning is that there is no "Make Things Better Quickly" plan. It's a shame because it would truly be a well-used mechanism. Making plans while struggling through our day-to-day is taxing, and often we feel more inclined to just stay in bed, or watch television, or participate in one of the many available vices that the world can offer.

However, as we are to be examples; furthermore, as we are called to be faithful, I suggest an alternative. Take everything you are doing, and give it to God. Let Him breathe into it, and become the instrument, rather than the conductor. The more that we can learn to let go of things, and put them in the control of the Almighty, the more we can learn how much better He does with those same things. Need an example? I can keep this one relatively simple: If you are reading this, it is only because I committed it to God. I am not good with marketing, or social media, but I am perfectly okay with writing in the hope of touching someone's heart, through God, and letting Him do whatever He would like to do with it.

Remember in your prayers today:

Lord, teach me to let You lead. Your plans are successful and leave no room for failure. I commit my works to You.

Aligning Desires with God's Will

- **Reflection**: Identify personal desires and align them with God's teachings.
- **Group Discussion or Journal**: How can we align our desires more closely with God's plan?

_____
_____
_____
_____
_____
_____
_____
_____
_____
_____
_____
_____
_____
_____
_____
_____
_____
_____
_____
_____
_____
_____
_____
_____
_____

Other passages to read when restoring faith:

"Then *Yeshua* said to them, "Where is your faith?" But they were afraid and marveled, saying to one another, "Who then is this? He commands even the winds and the water, and they obey Him!" Luke 8:25 (TLV)

"For His anger lasts for only a moment,
His favor is for a lifetime.
Weeping may stay for the night,
but joy comes in the morning." Psalm 30:6 (TLV)

"But He said to me, "My grace is sufficient for you, for power is made perfect in weakness." Therefore I will boast all the more gladly in my weaknesses, so that the power of Messiah may dwell in me. " 2 Corinthians 12:9 (TLV)

Day 18

SIIIIIooooowwww

*Know this, my dear brothers and sisters: let every person be quick
to listen, slow to speak, and slow to anger.*
Jacob (James) 1:19 (TLV)

Notes

_____

_____

_____

_____

_____

_____

_____

_____

I have noticed a consistency in men's nature that is extremely difficult to escape. We are built to respond and to act quickly. It is evidenced often in humanity's history where men jump to battle, to defend the homeland, or to address an oncoming attack. It could bear witness to a reason for anxiety when our marriages fail. We are so often focused on jumping into action, that we don't have the proper full view, resulting in loss.

71

James is encouraging us to pause. The scripture verse tells us that the only quickness that we should be seeking is to listen. The core difference in hearing and listening is that listening involves an act of submission. It causes us to put our immediate reactions and thoughts on a back burner to focus on what is being spoken to us.

Imagine if we truly lived by this scripture verse. How many situations that we are facing today would be handled better if we learned to keep a lid on our mouths and on our anger? It is never an easy thing to do. We are often filled to the brim with things we feel we are justified to say. There is always a point to be made or an argument to be won. Yet, the Bible teaches us that it isn't about that at all. We are called to be of a sound mind and to slow things down.

Challenge this verse within yourself today. Think back through the past week, or month, and ask yourself how many times you said something, and then wished you hadn't afterward. Sometimes we say it and it didn't even have a negative effect, but it had absolutely no effect. Let's treat our words with more honor, and our temperament as well. Speaking out of anger is a dangerous trap that can lead to the destruction of our relationships with every single person in our lives. Instead, keep a calm and quiet demeanor and observe. See what happens after that kind of response, and it nearly always will work out.

Remember in your prayers today:

Lord, teach me to be patient. Help me hold my tongue and to quiet my mind that I might listen. Let my responses be glorifying to You.

- **Challenge:** Spend a day focused on listening more than speaking.
- **Journal Reflection:** Note the impact of this exercise on understanding and relationships.

Other passages to read about patience:

"Better the end of a matter than its beginning. Better a patient spirit than a proud one." Ecclesiastes 7:8 (TLV)

"Love is patient,
love is kind,
it does not envy,
it does not brag,
it is not puffed up," 1 Corinthians 13:4 (TLV)

"You also be patient. Strengthen your hearts because the coming of the Lord is near." Jacob (James) 5:8 (TLV)

Day 19

Addition

But seek first the kingdom of God and His righteousness, and all these things shall be added to you. Therefore do not worry about tomorrow, for tomorrow will worry about itself. Each day has enough trouble of its own.
Matthew 6:33-34 (TLV)

Notes

_____

_____

_____

_____

_____

_____

_____

_____

_____

_____

_____

_____

_____

Every day is filled with a variety of mountains and valleys. Waking up is always the initial blessing, but who knows how the rest of the day will go? I have heard so many people state that if you approach every day with a good attitude, you will have nothing to worry about. However, when you are facing divorce, money issues, custody issues, work issues, social issues, etc. It is hard to jump out of bed with the "Let's rock this!" attitude.

We find scriptures like today's, where we are reminded to let tomorrow worry about itself. I understand the intensity of the sentiment, and it paints a beautiful picture of handing our worries over to God; yet, I can't help but wonder how often we actually adhere to this sort of thinking. Coming across different difficulties can become absolutely draining, and can leave us feeling empty.

So how do we embrace pushing through each days struggles? Well, we hope for a better tomorrow, and look for the little joys each day. The smile of one of your children, an unexpected hello, a cup of coffee. Those are moments that seem insignificant, but reflect the ability of God to still let a little sun shine through on the dark days.

Remember in your prayers today:

Thank you, Lord, for the little moments of joy or peace when everything feels so heavy.

Trusting in God's Provision

- **Activity**: Reflect on moments of worry and how trust in God's provision eased them.
- **Discussion or Journaling**: Share experiences of God's provision in times of need.

Other passages to read about thankfulness:

"I will praise ADONAI with my whole heart. I will tell about all Your wonders." Psalm 9:25 (TLV)

"I praise You in the great assembly, acclaiming You among a throng of people." Psalm 35:18 (TLV)

"Therefore as you received Messiah *Yeshua* as Lord, so continue to walk in Him—rooted and built up in Him and established in your faith just as you were taught, overflowing with thankfulness." Colossians 2:6-7 (TLV)

Day 20

The Troubled Heart

Do not let your heart be troubled. Trust in God; trust also in Me.
John 14:1 (TLV)

Notes

_____

_____

_____

_____

_____

_____

_____

_____

_____

_____

_____

_____

_____

_____

_____

_____

_____

_____

We often fall into a destructive pattern of trusting in the wrong people. It is almost human nature; Eve trusted the words of the serpent and it has spiraled ever since. With that trust, we almost always will end up having a troubled heart. Maybe a friendship meant more to you than it did to them, or maybe a marriage. In this season I have watched and witnessed family and friends go quiet, thinking that they are keeping the peace by just not speaking. This only exacerbates the heart condition of already feeling abandoned.

Yet, Yeshua is saying here to trust not only that God cares about you, but that the man Yeshua cares as well. As you continue to read in John 14, you will uncover that Yeshua is saying HE is the truth, the life, and the way. He is where our troubles go to be quelled.

Even if we feel like we are alone, another's sacrifice makes a way for us to find peace. He doesn't just desire to have peace in the next life but in this one. His promise here is true, if we lay out worry at his feet, then he will take on that burden.

Remember in your prayers today:

Thank you for caring enough about me that you will take on my troubles. Remind me of your love and mercy.

Dealing with a Troubled Heart

- **Exercise**: Write about a time your heart was troubled and how faith helped.
- **Prayer Focus**: Seek peace and trust in God for current troubles.

_____
_____
_____
_____
_____
_____
_____
_____
_____
_____
_____
_____
_____
_____
_____
_____
_____
_____
_____
_____
_____
_____
_____
_____
_____

Other passages to read when feeling worried:

"So I say to you, do not worry about your life—what you will eat or drink, or about your body, what you will wear. Isn't life more than food and the body more than clothing?" Matthew 6:25 (TLV)

"Fear not, for I am with you,
be not dismayed, for I am your God.
I will strengthen you.
Surely I will help you.
I will uphold you with My righteous right hand." Isaiah 41:10 (TLV)

"For God has not given us a spirit of timidity but of power and love and self-discipline." 2 Timothy 1:7 (TLV)

Day 21

What Is Love?

The righteous cry out and Adonai hears, and delivers them from all their troubles. Adonai is close to the brokenhearted, and saves those crushed in spirit.
Psalms 34:18-19 (TLV)

Notes

_____
_____
_____
_____
_____
_____
_____
_____
_____
_____
_____
_____
_____
_____
_____

As we face some of the most grueling and dark times of our lives, we may often feel like we are on a singular journey. We have the tendency to make ourselves the main character in the story of the universe. This mentality can lead to weighing ourselves down with a burden of responsibility for carrying every element of our own lives.

The Lord doesn't desire for us to be left wandering and holding our own baggage. As we walk through life, learning to place Him in control, we will discover that He actually cares. Today's passage shows us that there are benefits that come to those who are righteous. He hears those cries and groanings that we think no one else will care about.

He is a God who heals and restores. Learning from these moments of pain and despair is one of the many ways we can learn to have grace and mercy for others. He doesn't desire for us to hurt, but He knows that you can't be healed if you are always whole.

Remember in your prayers today:

Thank you, Lord, for listening to me when I cry out. Teach me to always seek righteousness, even when I am feeling at my lowest. Take these pieces of my heart and show me what beauty can be made from them.

Understanding Love

- **Reflection**: Contemplate how personal struggles have impacted your understanding of love.
- **Activity**: Journal about a time when you felt God's love during a tough moment.

_____
_____
_____
_____
_____
_____
_____
_____
_____
_____
_____
_____
_____
_____
_____
_____
_____
_____
_____
_____
_____
_____
_____
_____
_____

Other passages to read about love:

"Let all that you do be done in love." 1 Corinthians 16:14 (TLV)

"Fear not, for I am with you,
be not dismayed, for I am your God.
I will strengthen you.
Surely I will help you.
I will uphold you with My righteous right hand." Isaiah 41:10 (TLV)

"But above all these things put on love, which is the bond of perfect harmony." Colossians 3:14 (TLV)

Day 22

Restoration

He restores my soul. He guides me in paths of righteousness for His Name's sake.
Psalms 23:3 (TLV)

Notes

_____
_____
_____
_____
_____
_____
_____
_____
_____
_____
_____
_____
_____
_____
_____
_____
_____
_____
_____

A theme that comes up over and over in scripture when looking for encouragement and healing, is righteousness. They seemingly go hand-in-hand, where God makes the clear distinction that He is the source of both restoration and holiness.

There is a pruning that often needs to take place in our lives, just as a gardener would do to keep plants healthy. It is uncomfortable, often painful, and might even leave you wondering if it was worth it. The good news? It always is.

Pruning involves loss, which is a concept that we often recoil from. However, sometimes the loss of things is necessary to draw us to a more righteous walk with God. When things are lost to God, restoration can thrive. He never desires to leave us in a broken state, but rather to show His power and love through His capable grace.

Remember in your prayers today:

Lord, remind me that to lose myself is to gain more of You. Take those pieces and elements that I hold on to, that keep me from a closer walk with you, and purge them. Walk with me in the pain, and help me to remember that restoration is a process.

Embracing Restoration

- **Discussion Point:** Share how loss has led to personal growth and a deeper faith.
- **Prayer Focus**: Seek God's guidance in areas of life that need restoration.

_____
_____
_____
_____
_____
_____
_____
_____
_____
_____
_____
_____
_____
_____
_____
_____
_____
_____
_____
_____
_____
_____
_____

Other passages to read about integrity:

"The integrity of the upright guides them, but the crookedness of the treacherous will destroy them." Proverbs 11:3

"Yet with humility and reverence—keeping a clear conscience so that, whatever you are accused of, those who abuse you for your good conduct in Messiah may be put to shame." 1 Peter 3:16 (TLV)

"We have regard for what is honorable—not only before the Lord, but also before people." 2 Corinthians 8:21 (TLV)

Day 23

A Hope for Their Peace

All your children will be taught by Adonai.
Your children will have great shalom.
Isaiah 54:13 (TLV)

Notes

_____
_____
_____
_____
_____
_____
_____
_____
_____
_____
_____
_____
_____
_____
_____
_____

Facing divorce, custody, financial hardship, and uncertainty about the future can lead us to wonder what kind of life we are paving for our children. As father's, we should desire the best for them in every aspect of their lives. Still, we know that our parents thought the same for us, and we are now here facing these trials that we never saw coming.

This is the importance of recognizing that God has provided us with the things we need to help our children realize that they are only going to be successful through Him. Sure, there are those street-smart lessons that we can teach them, but what about the core of who we are? Those are elements of God that are spoken about in scripture as a way to guide us. He desires our children to love and uphold His Word. He desires for them to speak peace and to have the same for themselves.

Allowing God, through His Word, to become their teacher will equip them for a future that shows them where to place their trust where it can never fail. They will learn where the source of peace and love really comes from. They will know that no matter what they face, God desires wholeness.

Remember in your prayers today:

Commit me to teach Your Word, Lord. Remind me that how You speak to me, You can speak to them. My hope rests in You, as should theirs.

Peace for Children

- **Parenting Exercise:** Plan ways to teach children about finding peace through faith.
- **Reflection:** Consider how faith influences your approach to parenting.

Other passages to read about peace:

"Finally, brothers and sisters, rejoice! Aim for restoration, encourage one another, be of the same mind, live in *shalom*—and the God of love and *shalom* will be with you."
2 Corinthians 13:11 (TLV)

"These things I have spoken to you, so that in Me you may have *shalom*. In the world you will have trouble, but take heart! I have overcome the world!" John 16:33 (TLV)

"I will lie down and sleep in *shalom*. For You alone, ADONAI, make me live securely." Psalm 4:9 (TLV)

Day 24

Beware The Envy

A tranquil heart is life to the body,
but envy is rottenness to the bones.
Proverbs 14:30 (TLV)

Notes

_____

_____
_____
_____
_____
_____
_____
_____
_____
_____
_____
_____
_____
_____
_____
_____
_____
_____
_____

Perhaps one of the most aggravating elements of divorce and separation is the feeling of loss. Sometimes we misplace that feeling with anger. Anger over a loss of money, or time spent with your children, or even just the loss of feelings. We might even find ourselves wondering why the other person should have it so good when we are being torn apart.

This is how envy works. It makes you question your decisions, to second guess things that even God helped bring you to. We can't see the future, so we look to what others have and compare ourselves to it. It's a slippery slope that will toss us down into a pit of self-destruction. We take things personally because that is part of our nature.

Consider replacing those feelings with a desire to know God more deeply. I have found throughout these months of hardships, that chasing after a better relationship with God has changed my feelings about love, wants, and needs. I have found that He takes things away, and He restores them. If I had been too blinded by envy to consider seeking more of God, I know that I would be eaten up with bitterness and grasping for things that won't benefit myself or my children.

Remember in your prayers today:

Help me flee from envy. I want to rely on you, Lord. I want to know you better. Consume my thoughts and hold my heart.

Overcoming Envy

- **Self-Reflection**: Identify moments of envy and strategize on how to focus on God's blessings instead.
- **Journal Prompt**: Write about the impact of envy on spiritual and emotional well-being.

_____
_____
_____
_____
_____
_____
_____
_____
_____
_____
_____
_____
_____
_____
_____
_____
_____
_____
_____
_____
_____
_____
_____
_____

Other passages to read when feeling envious:

"Do not let your heart envy sinners, but always be in the fear of ADONAI." Proverbs 23:17 (TLV)

"So get rid of all malice and all deceit and hypocrisy and envy and all *lashon ha-ra*." 1 Peter 2:1 (TLV)

"For where jealousy and selfish ambition exist, there is disorder and every evil practice." James 3:16 (TLV)

Day 25

Note Your Desires

*But each one is tempted when he is dragged away
and enticed by his own desire.*
Jacob (James) 1:14 (TLV)

Notes

_____
_____
_____
_____
_____
_____
_____
_____
_____
_____
_____
_____
_____
_____
_____
_____

How hopeless would we be if we let ourselves give into our desires? Think of the various selfish thoughts that we have through each day. How about those times we just want to give someone a piece of our mind? What of the moments where we start thinking about vices that we think will fix our feelings?

Allow me to be clear: we do not know what is best for ourselves. We are selfish creatures who rely so often on self-preservation. Noticing this mindset is the critical first step that God wants us to be aware of. Every one of us will have these thoughts and desires, but we are called to replace them with holiness.

This means that God is willing and capable of curbing our selfish appetites. When you are struggling, pray, and read the Word. There is something in there for you. Following every emotional impulse leads us to loneliness and depression.

Change your reliance. It is hard to do, but it is so necessary. Learn to replace your desires with His, and watch what He can do.

Remember in your prayers today:

Tear me away from my own desires. Teach me to think of You, and Your heart. Use me as a vessel to do Your will.

Controlling Desires

- **Challenge**: Practice self-discipline in areas of personal desire.
- **Group Discussion or Journaling**: Discuss the impact of desires on spiritual life.

Other passages to read about desire:

"You open Your hand and satisfy every living thing with favor." Psalm 145:16 (TLV)

"He will fulfill the desire of those who fear Him. He will hear their cry and save them." Psalm 145:19 (TLV)

"The desire of the righteous is only good, but the hope of the wicked only wrath." Proverbs 11:23 (TLV)

Day 26

The Jealous One

But if you have bitter jealousy and selfish ambition in your heart, do not boast and lie against the truth. This is not the wisdom that comes down from above, but is earthly, unspiritual, demonic. For where jealousy and selfish ambition exist, there is disorder and every evil practice. But the wisdom that is from above is first pure, then peaceable, gentle, open to reason, full of mercy and good fruits, impartial, not hypocritical.
Jacob (James) 3:14-17 (TLV)

Notes

_____
_____
_____
_____
_____
_____
_____
_____
_____
_____
_____

We live in a time where evil is viewed as relative, or some kind of literary device that writers use to portray an antagonist. However, evil is very real and very present. It takes no longer than 30 seconds of a nightly news segment to realize that there is active evil unless we disassociate from that as well.

Jealousy is often reflected on and brought up in discussions of struggling romances, but it can be present in any aspect of life. It occurs consistently in the desire to one-up each other, which is why I bring it up in this devotional. There will be times when your children's other parent does something that causes jealousy to rise up. Maybe they picked a "better" vacation or got them a "better" gift. We can get wrapped up in our feelings and forget to realize that what our kids actually need is us. They need to feel loved and supported. It has nothing to do with the "things" we can provide them.

Beware of allowing evil to control your responsibility, God wants no part of it. He desires order and peace, which are only found through Him.

Remember in your prayers today:

Lord, provide me peace and the endurance to fight against jealousy and selfishness. Replace my feelings with Your love.

attling Jealousy

- **Activity**: Reflect on situations where jealousy arose and how it was addressed.
- **Prayer Focus**: Pray for strength to replace jealousy with contentment and love.

Other passages to read about jealousy:

"For jealousy enrages a man and he will show no mercy in the day of revenge." Proverbs 6:34 (TLV)

"A tranquil heart is life to the body, but envy is rottenness to the bones." Proverbs 14:30 (TLV)

"For where jealousy and selfish ambition exist, there is disorder and every evil practice." James 3:16 (TLV)

Day 27

The Arrogant

Arrogance yields nothing but strife. Wisdom belongs to those who take advice.
Proverbs 13:10 (TLV)

Notes

_____

_____

_____

_____

_____

_____

_____

_____

_____

_____

_____

_____

_____

_____

_____

_____

_____

_____

We tend to have main character syndrome pretty severely when we are facing stress and heartache. It becomes easy to begin treating everyone else like an NPC (non-playable character). Yet, God warns us that our arrogance will only get us into conflict.

I have thought about that statement quite a bit and always thought about it in the sense of other people warring against us because we are so dangerously self-centered. What was revealed to me, however, is that most of that strife is internalized. Think of your worst moments of arrogance.

Typically, it stems from feeling like an injustice has been done against you, and that no one can possibly understand your viewpoint. So, rather than listen to anyone else, we boil in our own cauldron of self-defeating mentality.

Sometimes things just plain suck. Other times an injustice really has been done.

The close to today's passage point blank tells us that we should be open to hearing others out. Tearing open our selfishness is the only way to defeat the pain that arrogance will lead us to. What kind of life would we live if we were so wrapped up in ourselves that we couldn't recognize the hurt that others are going through? Arrogance plays in so many different forms, but we are told to unite with others to defeat it.

Remember in your prayers today:

Lord, remind me constantly that I am not the center of this universe. Empower me to listen to others, and to be there when they need me.

onfronting Arrogance

- **Exercise**: Identify instances of arrogance and consider their impacts on relationships.
- **Reflection**: Explore the importance of humility in spiritual growth.

Other passages to read about integrity:

"The integrity of the upright guides them, but the crookedness of the treacherous will destroy them." Proverbs 11:3

"Yet with humility and reverence—keeping a clear conscience so that, whatever you are accused of, those who abuse you for your good conduct in Messiah may be put to shame." 1 Peter 3:16 (TLV)

"We have regard for what is honorable—not only before the Lord, but also before people." 2 Corinthians 8:21 (TLV)

Day 28

The Hardest Virtue

We pray that you may be strengthened with all the power that comes from His glorious might, for you to have all kinds of patience and steadfastness...
Colossians 1:11 (TLV)

Notes
_____
_____
_____
_____
_____
_____
_____
_____
_____
_____
_____
_____
_____
_____
_____
_____

If there is one thing that completely overloads my internal system and I mean to the point of nearly shutting me down, it is being late. I can feel my body yelling from its core if I even think I might not be somewhere on time. I understand that some things are more important than others, but the anxiety I feel is the same no matter what rung on the ladder the task may be.

Now, I know that this comes directly from my impatience, and it has been an ongoing battle for years. Waiting for someone to answer a question, or even for someone to finish telling their story can sometimes be excruciating. I have at least learned to internalize it, which gives me different problems.

Scriptures like today's remind me that we all need champions praying for us. I am blessed to have a mother who is constant in intercession. I think every one of us should seek out those who will pray for us to be strengthened in patience.

It is especially important as a parent, and even more so when going through custody battles. It can feel so overwhelming when such important aspects of your life are wrapped up in phone calls or emails between lawyers. That is where impatience and fall into anger. Find your support, find prayer partners, and keep yourself prayerfully minded as well.

Remember in your prayers today:

Forgive me, Lord. I know that I so often neglect the lessons you are teaching. Keep me strong as I face these trials, that you might be glorified in my patience.

Cultivating Patience

- **Patience Challenge**: Set daily goals to practice patience in difficult situations.
- **Journal Prompt**: Note experiences and feelings when practicing patience.

_____
_____
_____
_____
_____
_____
_____
_____
_____
_____
_____
_____
_____
_____
_____
_____
_____
_____
_____
_____
_____
_____
_____
_____
_____
_____

Other passages to read about peace:

"Finally, brothers and sisters, rejoice! Aim for restoration, encourage one another, be of the same mind, live in *shalom*—and the God of love and *shalom* will be with you."
2 Corinthians 13:11 (TLV)

"These things I have spoken to you, so that in Me you may have *shalom*. In the world you will have trouble, but take heart! I have overcome the world!" John 16:33 (TLV)

"I will lie down and sleep in *shalom*. For You alone, ADONAI, make me live securely." Psalm 4:9 (TLV)

Day 29

The Key

Hear O Israel, the Lord our God, the Lord is one. Love Adonai your God with all your heart and with all your soul and with all your strength.
Deuteronomy 6:4-5 (TLV)

Notes

_____
_____
_____
_____
_____
_____
_____
_____
_____
_____
_____
_____
_____
_____
_____

Today's passage is one of the most important scripture verses that serve as a basis for our faith. These scriptures were the first thing said to my daughter right after she was born. Happily, it is also the first passage that she has memorized.

How do they apply to our struggles as parents facing trials, court decisions, financial burdens, lost time with our children etc...? We should never forget our purpose, or who we are in Christ. We were created to worship Him, to glorify him no matter the situation. During these hard times, it is our love for God that will help sustain us.

Our hearts can break, our will can break, and our emotions can spike in every different direction. Yet, God has never changed. What's more, is that He has also promised us that He has already overcome the world.

No matter our brokenness, we are still required to love Him with everything that we are. I can speak from experience, that this will get you through absolute chaos.

I have been brought through turmoil in the last few months, but have clung to the recognition of who I am in Christ. Even when others portray you in a ravenous or defamatory way, your relationship with God is the ultimate truth. Take heart that it can never be taken away from you. Continue to chase after God and discover a deeper relationship with Him.

Remember in your prayers today:

You created me, and You love me. Let me words and heart be subject to Your will.

Emphasizing God's Love

- **Reflection**: Focus on how loving God with all your heart has helped in difficult times.
- **Activity**: Create a list of ways to strengthen your relationship with God.

_____
_____
_____
_____
_____
_____
_____
_____
_____
_____
_____
_____
_____
_____
_____
_____
_____
_____
_____
_____
_____
_____
_____
_____

Other passages to read about truth:

"And He said to him, "'You shall love *ADONAI* your God with all your heart, and with all your soul, and with all your mind.' This is the first and greatest commandment. " Matthew 22:37-38 (TLV)

"We are from God; whoever knows God listens to us, but whoever is not from God does not listen to us. By this we know the Spirit of truth and the spirit of error." 1 John 4:6 (TLV)

"Make every effort to present yourself before God as tried and true, as an unashamed worker cutting a straight path with the word of truth." 2 Timothy 2:15 (TLV)

Day 30

The Hope

These things I have spoken to you, so that in Me you may have shalom. In the world you will have trouble, but take heart! I have overcome the world!
John 16:33 (TLV)

Notes

_____
_____
_____
_____
_____
_____
_____
_____
_____
_____

It is my prayer that these last thirty days have been filled with a real relationship with God. I am hopeful that everyone who went on this journey looked at themselves, and their faith, and discovered that despite all of these struggles, He is still a present and loving God.

Today's passage was chosen first, and I knew that the words they speak bring constant peace.

God wants the best for each of us, even if that involves the pruning process. Sometimes every wall and safety net has to be purged to bring us back into a relationship with the Almighty.

Our peace can only come from Him because it is the only peace that isn't temporary. I know that most people's journeys are not complete within thirty days and that many of us are still facing hardships and battles. I waited until after I was brought through the court process to write this.

To be the most raw, right here at the end, I would love to tell you that everything worked out. However, it didn't. There were losses, relationships damaged, and falsities spoken. I have been torn down to my core, and I know now that I needed to be.

You see, this devotional was written during all of the pain, not after. Every scripture was chosen because it is what I was feeling and facing at the moment. If you read one and identify with it, it is because we are human...together.

I will leave you with this: there is nothing without Christ. He is the only sustainer, provider, and comfort that can bring you through every single circumstance. Stay strong in the Lord, and let Him renew you a little more each day.

Remember in your prayers today:

Lord, bless every person who is going through battles. Let them feel your loving arms wrapped around them. Continue to guide us and lead us after Your will.

Finding Peace in Christ

- **Closing Reflection**: Summarize how the devotional journey has impacted your faith and life.
- **Prayer Activity**: Write a prayer of thanks for God's guidance through trials.

_____
_____
_____
_____
_____
_____
_____
_____
_____
_____
_____
_____
_____
_____
_____
_____
_____
_____
_____
_____
_____
_____
_____
_____
_____

Other passages to read about truth:

"*Yeshua* said to him, "I am the way, the truth, and the life! No one comes to the Father except through Me." John 14:6

"We are from God; whoever knows God listens to us, but whoever is not from God does not listen to us. By this we know the Spirit of truth and the spirit of error." 1 John 4:6 (TLV)

"Make every effort to present yourself before God as tried and true, as an unashamed worker cutting a straight path with the word of truth." 2 Timothy 2:15 (TLV)

TOPICAL CONTENT

It was always my desire for this book to be reusable, and to help even after the 30 days are completed. This list compiles the different topics covered, for whenever you need to revisit them.

Emotional Management:
Anger (Days 2, 5)
Worry (Day 4)
Jealousy (Day 26)
Envy (Day 24)

Personal Growth and Integrity:
Heart and Spirituality (Days 1, 10)
Integrity (Day 3)
Progress and Perseverance (Days 6, 7, 12, 14)
Patience (Day 18)
Desire (Day 25)

Relationships and Social Dynamics:
Fatherhood and Parenting (Days 9, 16)
Equality and Arrogance (Days 8, 27)
Love (Day 21)
Praise and Gratitude (Days 11, 19)

Faith and Spirituality:
Trials and Endurance (Days 13, 15)
Planning and Restoring Faith (Days 17, 22)
Key to Faith (Days 29, 30)

Peace and Heart Matters:
Troubled Heart (Day 20)
Peace (Days 23, 28)

Made in the USA
Middletown, DE
06 September 2024